GOLF

Written By:
Herbert I. Kavet

Illustrated By:
Martin Riskin

Manufactured in the United States of America

30 29 28 27 26 25 24 23 22 21 20 19 18 17 16 15 14 13 12 11 10 9 8 7 6 5 4

Ivory Tower Publishing Co., Inc.
111 Bauer Drive
Oakland, N.J. 07436

Really fine golf courses have distances marked on
the sprinkler heads.

Golf Equipment

A good golfer can play an adequate game with any old rusty set of clubs found lying in the garage. There are, however, two good reasons for having the latest equipment besides currying favor with the pro at the golf shop.

1. To intimidate your opponent, which will probably work up to the point of your first swing.

2. So you have something to blame when shots go wrong.

Golf Equipment

This second reason is the basis for the entire golf equipment industry giving gainful employment to millions of people. Blaming equipment naturally includes throwing, losing, banging and bashing—activities that keep those golf factories humming and have stopped the recession from having any effect at all in seven states.

The Psychological Game

Don't make the mistake of spending lots of time practicing to improve your game. It's much more efficient to learn to neutralize your opponent's game with psychological warfare. Golf is a game of concentration and if you break your opponent's concentration, you destroy his game.

The Psychological Game

"How do you do this?" you say. It's easy. With an overweight player or anyone on a diet, talk about food. "Hey, Harry, how about some Chinese food after the game?" If your rival is having a great day, just comment on his or her stroke. "Swing looks fabulous today, Carol. What are you doing different?" Once she starts to think about it, the smooth play will all vanish. If someone is using a new piece of equipment, clubs, gloves, or shoes, you have only to comment, "Say, Bill, those new gloves broken in yet?..." You get the picture.

How To Go In The Woods

The call of nature usually hits between the 6th and 7th hole stimulated by that extra cup of coffee and the excitement of a birdie on the 5th hole. It's nice to have some shrubs around at this time, but not so thick as to cause scratches when you slip into the woods. Men have a natural advantage for certain functions and if they point cleverly with their hands, even when in the open, most people will think they are indicating some unusual bird or locating a lost ball.

How To Go In The Woods

There are 3 approved methods for more serious operations in the woods, if you know what I mean. The sitting on a log method seems closest to home, but no one in the history of golf has ever found a suitable log in a suitable place. The hanging from a tree is good if you've got strong arms; and the back against a tree is quite comfortable if you can manage to miss your dropped pants with the business end of the whole exercise.

Sid listened to the pro and kept his head down.
Somebody stole his golf cart.

Driving Range

The driving range is the sadistic relief center for golf. Here is where golfers line up to try to hit some poor unfortunate, locked in a steel cage built around an old jeep. The guy who picks up balls in this contraption is usually a former caddy who talked too much about his client's indiscretions of scoring—most golfers feel this punishment is too light.

Roger and Bennett discuss their scores
on the 14th hole.

Marc lines up what later proves to be the last shot of his game.

Since Ron got the new turbocharged golf cart, he
never has to play a bad lie.

Scott's overswing finally responds to chiropractic care.

Lost Clubs

The caddy who keeps all his client's misdeeds an absolute secret is promoted to clean-up maintenance man. He gets to pick up all the lost clubs that are left around greens and is usually the richest man at the club.

How To Tell A Real Golfer

1. Real golfers never hit their caddy with an iron.

2. Real golfers never get poison ivy.

3. Real golfers never pass out at the 19th hole.

How To Tell A Real Golfer

4. Real golfers don't let their kids drive their golf carts.

5. Real golfers don't use tees shaped like naked women.

6. Real golfers don't cry when they miss a one-handed tap in.

OUR IVORY TOWER PRODUCTS PROVIDE A COMICAL AND WHIMSICAL INSIGHT INTO OUR EVERYDAY LIVES.

OTHER POPULAR ITEMS AVAILABLE AT MANY FINE STORES INCLUDE:

- TRADE PAPER BACK BOOKS
- FUN BOOKS
- PLAYING CARDS
- JOURNALS

IVORY TOWER PUBLISHING CO.,INC.,
111 BAUER DRIVE,
OAKLAND, N.J. 07436